HIKING GUIDE

TO

DELAWARE WATER GAP

NATIONAL RECREATION AREA

Revised Edition
1994

by Nick Miskowski

Edited by
Daniel D. Chazin

Page Design and Makeup by
Alice L. Tufel

Cover Design by
Steve Butfilowski

Cover Photograph by
Michael Warren

Published by
The New York-New Jersey Trail Conference
GPO Box 2250 ○ New York NY 10116 ○ 212/685-9699

Library of Congress Cataloging-in-Publication Data

Miskowski, Nick, 1953-
Hiking guide to Delaware Water Gap National
Recreation Area / by Nick Miskowski ; edited by
Daniel D. Chazin. -- Rev. ed.
    p. cm.
Rev. ed. of: Hiking guide to Delaware Water Gap National
Recreation Area / by Michael Steele. Rev. ed. c1991.
    ISBN 1-880775-01-8
    1. Hiking--Delaware Water Gap National Recreation
Area (N.J. and Pa.)--Guidebooks. 2. Delaware Water
Gap National Recreation Area (N.J. and Pa.)--
Guidebooks. I. Chazin, Daniel D. II. Steele, Michael.
Hiking guide to   Delaware Water Gap National
Recreation Area. III. Title.
GV199.42.D43S74 1994
796.5'1'0974822--dc20   94-21406 CIP

The Conference is a federation of 82 hiking and environmental organiza-
tions and 9,000+ individuals dedicated to building and maintaining
hiking trails and protecting the related openspace in the bi-state region.
Our volunteers maintain over 1,000 miles of marked hiking trails
including the 300+ mile Long Path and the NY and NJ sections of the
Appalachian Trail. Our network includes in NY: the Catskills, Taconics,
Fahnestock, Hudson Highlands, Minnewaska, Harriman-Bear Mtn.,
Schunemunk, Storm King, Black Rock Forest and the Staten Island
Greenbelt ... and in NJ: the Ramapos, Wyanokies, Kittatinnies, Palisades
and other natural areas of Bergen, Passaic, Sussex, Warren and Morris
Counties. Membership includes a subscription to our bi-monthly *Trail
Walker* as well as 20-25% discounts on our maps/guides and an
extensive discount program with area outdoor stores and lodges. Dues
start at just $12⁵⁰. For information on membership, publications and
volunteer opportunities, please write or call (anytime).

Contents

PREFACE

This book, a guide to the trails in the Delaware Water Gap National Recreation Area and the adjacent Worthington State Forest, is the successor to the book by the same name published in 1986 by Michael Steele, a revised edition of which was published by the New York-New Jersey Trail Conference in 1991. This edition builds upon the fine work of Michael Steele, and includes changes and updates that have occurred since the last edition of his book was published. The maps in this guide were drawn by Michael Steele, and have been updated as necessary.

I would like to extend my sincere appreciation to all who assisted me with the revision of this guide—Andrew P. Wiggins, Brent Garrison, Andrew Garrison, George Brown, Dennis Goodenough, and especially Harry Hoyd for his computer expertise. I would like also to thank Daniel D. Chazin, Publications Chairman of the New York-New Jersey Trail Conference, for his help in editing the book, and Richard J. Kavalek, who measured some of the trails, especially in Worthington State Forest. Finally, I wish to express my thanks to the staff of the National Park Service at

Delaware Water Gap National Recreation Area, and especially Randy W. Turner, Chief of Visitor Services, for their valuable insights, which contributed to this revision.

This book is dedicated to my son Andrew — may he find adventure and challenge in the great outdoors.

NICK MISKOWSKI

INTRODUCTION

The Delaware Water Gap National Recreation Area includes nearly 70,000 acres of public land managed for recreational use—open space for everyone to enjoy. In managing this area, the National Park Service tries both to provide for recreational enjoyment by the public and to preserve the quality of resources for future generations. Within the boundaries of the National Recreation Area, but managed separately by the State of New Jersey, is Worthington State Forest. This land is also managed for public recreation and is patrolled by State Park rangers.

There also are scattered parcels of private land within the National Recreation Area. Please respect the rights of private owners, and do not trespass on land posted as private property.

To ensure harmony among recreational visitors and to keep the resources from deteriorating, various regulations have been enacted. For example: camping and fires are permitted only at designated areas, and alcohol is prohibited at Worthington State Forest campsites and several posted sites within the Delaware Water Gap National Recreation Area.

If you have any questions about rules pertaining to your particular interests, ask one of the rangers who patrol the area, or stop by one of the visitor centers for helpful information.

HISTORY

This river valley region between the Pocono Mountains and the Kittatinny Ridge has experienced extensive geological and cultural change.

Before Europeans ventured up the Delaware in the early 17th century, the Lenape (Delaware) Indians lived in harmony with the land and waters. The Kittatinny and Minisink region was, for them, "land of the chiefs"—a place of bountiful wildlife and rich, alluvial soil for their humble crops of maize, squash, and beans. The corruption and eventual destruction of their culture has been well documented; by 1801, only a few Lenape remained in their ancestral homeland.

The Lenape were usurped first by the Dutch, who began searching for minerals, primarily copper and iron, in the mid-1600's. The copper mines and Old Mine Road may have been originally engineered by these hearty and resourceful explorers. A number of them befriended and exchanged knowledge with the Lenape. But the pressure of additional Europeans over the following decades, and the establishment of several small towns north of the Water Gap by the early 1800's, ultimately eroded the vestiges of Indian culture.

The river had long been the central means of transportation for both natives and Europeans. In addition to following the main stream, settlers needed to cross the Delaware. A number of ferries provided this service. Though no ferries currently operate within the Recreation Area, their names, such as

Dingmans, persist. Bridges now span most sites where flatboat ferries once poled.

Other transportation through and in the vicinity of the Gap gradually superseded the river. Railroads were built in the mid-1800's. A small town on the Pennsylvania side of the river changed its name from Dutotsville to Delaware Water Gap. People drawn here from metropolitan areas by the natural beauty and spectacular geological landmark visited the elegant hotels and smaller inns that were established throughout the area, primarily in the Poconos. The resort business declined prior to World War II, and most of the old hotels are long gone. But they were replaced by a surge of new hotel, resort, and second-home development after Route 80 was constructed through the Gap in the late 1950's.

Today, the Recreation Area provides a precious natural island in the midst of burgeoning development. The pristine and mighty Delaware River, with its landmark Gap, is now a refreshing recreational focus for the large urban populations nearby.

How did the river open the gap in the ridge? To answer this question, you need to do a little geological time travel over a span of 400 million years when this region was a part of a broad flat plain interlaced with meandering streams. Gradually, as the sea level rose, a shallow ocean compressed the alluvium from those streams, converting it to sedimentary rock, such as the shale common in this region. Two hundred million years ago, this substrate was uplifted and folded to form the Appalachian Mountains, monstrous peaks, perhaps more impressive than the Himalayas at one time. As this folding proceeded, a major river continued to find its way through openings and erodible strata until what we call a "water gap" in the mountain was formed. This process is still continuing today. Erosion, weathering, and two million years of glacial activity modified and shrank the Appalachians and deposited rocks, boulders, and glacial silt from northern latitudes. The results of glaciation are most obviously seen in the boulder fields along the Kittatinny Mountains, lakes such as Sunfish Pond, and waterfalls.

In 1962, Congress passed the Flood Control Act, which authorized the construction of a dam at Tocks Island. In 1965, President Johnson signed into law the Act authorizing the Delaware Water Gap National Recreation Area. But public opposition put a halt to the construction of the dam, which would have turned this section of the Delaware into a 40-mile-long reservoir. The National Park Service now manages the land to preserve the natural and cultural resources and provide for recreational pursuits.

TRAILS, TRAILS, AND TRAILS

There are trails, and then there are trails, many of which are depicted in this guide. Trail conditions vary greatly. Some of the trails described are officially maintained either by the Park or by volunteer organizations, such as the New York-New Jersey Trail Conference. Others are not maintained, and are merely suggested hiking routes. Some of them are easy, while others are fairly rugged. Several are well engineered, but most are quite "natural." When you hike on a trail that is not maintained, you may only be following a trodden path through the forest and mountain terrain, so be prepared. If you are not an experienced hiker, we suggest that you hike on the official, maintained trails. Wear good hiking shoes and use common sense. Don't attempt steep terrain beyond your ability. Stay on the trail, and remember that off-trail hiking in certain areas may result in damage to the natural resources, including soil erosion, disturbance of wildlife habitats, and injury to threatened or endangered plants. Use the descriptions in this book as a guide, but remember that trail routes, blazes, and hence descriptions may change over time.

EQUIPMENT, MAPS, AND COMMON SENSE

Equipment

Equipment requirements will vary, depending upon weather conditions, your physical stamina, the length and duration of the hike, and the topography of the trails. Suggested items include hiking boots, insect repellent, rain gear, handkerchief, notebook and pencil, whistle, first-aid kit, small backpack, hiking guide, sunscreen, waterproof matches, flashlight, food and water.

Maps

The maps in this guide are *not* drawn to scale, and are provided as a supplement to the written descriptions. Please refer to both when hiking the trails. The New York-New Jersey Trail Conference has produced a series of fine maps of this area that provide greater detail, including contour lines. These maps (and USGS topographic maps, which provide more detail but often do not correctly show trail routes) may be purchased at private outfitters and at the National Park Service visitor centers.

The following symbols are used on the maps in this guide:

trail   ------   old road   = = = = = =

stream   ~·~·~·   parking   P

Common Sense

A word to the wise—please inform someone *where* you plan to hike, *what route* you plan to take, and *when* you plan to return (and stick with your plan). As with any outdoor pursuit, the unexpected can happen, and as the old adage goes, an ounce of prevention is worth a pound of cure. Although rangers are well trained in rescue operations, please do not require them to demonstrate their skills. Water sources along the trails may dry up at times, and all water taken from unprotected sources should be purified before using. Most hikers will want to bring ample water with them. Please respect the rights of private property owners, follow park regulations (they are designed to protect visitors and preserve resources for future enjoyment), be safe, and enjoy.

PICNIC AREAS AND BOAT LAUNCHES

Several public-use areas are located in Pennsylvania and New Jersey within the Recreation Area. Maps depicting their locations are available at the Park Headquarters and visitor centers.

New Jersey

From the southern end of the park at the Delaware Water Gap, the Old Mine Road wanders northward, offering views of the Delaware River, mountains and waterfalls. The following areas are listed from south to north and are accessible from the Old Mine Road:

Kittatinny Point. Visitor center, boat launch, river fishing, picnic area, and a spectacular view of the Delaware Water Gap.

Poxono Boat Launch. River access for small trailered boats and cartops.

Depew Recreation Site. Picnic area, open areas for ball and frisbee playing, kite flying, river fishing, and access for cartop boats.

Van Campens Glen. This area is shaded by hemlock and rhododendron that border Van Campens Brook, and features a small picnic area and a natural trout stream fishing area. Special fishing regulations apply.

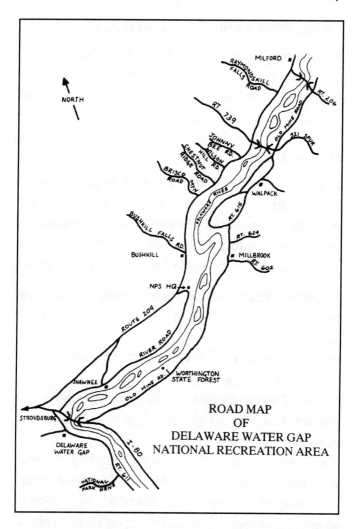

ROAD MAP
OF
DELAWARE WATER GAP
NATIONAL RECREATION AREA

Watergate. A series of ponds provide for fishing, and a natural trout stream fishing area is nearby. There is a large picnic area, with open areas for ball and frisbee playing. Restrooms and water are available.

Millbrook Village. Picnic tables, restrooms, water and public telephones are available in this reconstructed village. Weddings have been held in the church in the off-seasons (by permit only). A natural trout stream fishing area is nearby.

Pennsylvania

From the southern end of the park at the Delaware Water Gap, River Road heads north to Route 209 in Bushkill, offering views of the mountains, farmlands and the Delaware River.

Overlooks. Three overlooks along Route 611, south of the village of Delaware Water Gap, offer spectacular views of the Water Gap. A short walk from Point of Gap Overlook offers river fishing.

Hialeah Picnic Area. North of Shawnee on River Road, Hialeah offers individual picnic areas. Alcohol is not permitted.

Smithfield Beach. This high-use area offers a lifeguarded swimming beach in the summer months,

canoe and boat launches, river fishing, and a picnic area with open areas for ball and frisbee playing and kite flying. The area is handicapped accessible, and barrier-free restrooms are available, as well as water and public telephones. Alcohol is not permitted.

Hidden Lake. Located on Hidden Lake Drive off of River Road, this 17-acre lake offers a beach, picnic area, bank fishing, and cartop boating. (Boat fishing is not permitted on this lake.)

Bushkill Access Area. North of Bushkill on Route 209, this area offers a boat launch and river fishing.

Toms Creek. To reach this area, take the first left from Route 209 north of the Bushkill access. There is a quiet picnic area along Toms Creek and fishing in the stream. Special fishing regulations apply.

Eshback Access Area. From Route 209, a gravel road across from white barns leads to a small trailered boat access with river fishing and blanket picnicking.

Loch Lomond Pond. From Route 209 in Dingmans Ferry, follow Wilson Hill Road to the pond, which features a small picnic area and offers fishing.

Dingmans Falls. Follow signs from Route 209 at Dingmans Ferry. This area offers a visitor center, picnic area, stream fishing and trails to Silver Thread and Dingmans Falls.

Dingmans Access. Follow signs from Route 209 at Dingmans Ferry. This area offers boat and canoe access and river fishing.

George W. Childs Recreation Site. Follow signs from Route 209. A short walk on wooden stairs and bridges leads to beautiful views of several waterfalls among the hemlocks and rhododendron. Picnic tables are available.

Milford Beach. Follow signs from Route 209 just south of Milford. This area offers a lifeguarded swimming beach in the summer months, a picnic shelter, boat and canoe launches, river fishing, and open areas for ball and frisbee playing and kite flying. Handicapped-accessible, barrier-free restrooms are available.

NEW JERSEY

TRAILS

RED DOT TRAIL

1.3 miles

Location: Park at the Rest Area off of I-80, or you can park at the Dunnfield Creek Parking Area or the Kittatinny Point Visitor Center and walk to the Rest Area.

The Red Dot Trail leads to the top of Mt. Tammany. It is a highly popular trail, scenic with sweeping views, and is quite steep and rugged. The uphill march is unrelenting, but the commanding view from the rocks at the summit looking way down to The Gap and the Delaware River is a famous scenic view.

The trail starts at the Rest Area by the sign and follows red-on-white blazes. You will soon start slowing down because the trail is steep. After 0.4 mile, the trail moves over to the bluff overlooking I-80, soon reaching an excellent viewpoint, which provides a good place to rest. From here, the trail follows a rocky rib away from the bluff, crosses a wet spot, carefully makes its way up a rocky slab, and crosses an area with boulders.

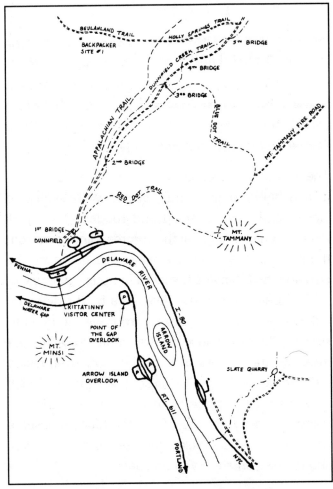

Red Dot Trail and Blue Dot Trail

After a little more uphill hiking, the trail reaches the summit (1,549 feet). The rocky viewpoint is just down to your right. The blue blazes of the Blue Dot Trail start here; you may want to follow them back down to make a 3.5-mile loop hike.

Mt. Tammany is a natural area and extremely popular as a day hike. Camping is not permitted. Please do not litter; carry your litter down to the garbage receptacles at the parking area.

BLUE DOT TRAIL 1.8 miles	*Location: Park at Dunnfield Creek Parking Area off I-80.*

This trail leads more gradually to the top of Mt. Tammany. It is often hiked in conjunction with the Red Dot Trail as a loop hike. To reach the Blue Dot Trail, first follow the Appalachian Trail along Dunnfield Creek for 0.4 mile to where the A.T. veers off to the left. The blue-blazed Blue Dot Trail starts here (along with the green-blazed Dunnfield Creek Trail) and continues straight ahead, following the creek for a short distance. The trail then turns right and crosses the creek on a footbridge. In another 300 feet, the Blue Dot Trail turns right, leaving the Dunn-field Creek Trail, and starts its uphill trudge along a rough old roadbed to the ridgetop. At 1.5 miles, it reaches the ridge at an intersection with the Mt. Tammany Fire Road. The Blue Dot Trail turns sharply right and follows along the ridge for 0.3 mile to meet the Red Dot Trail at Mt. Tammany's scenic lookout.

BEULAHLAND TRAIL
1.3 miles

Location: Park at the Farview Parking Area, on the right side of Old Mine Road, a mile north of the I-80 bridge. (The Karamac Parking Area is across the road on the left.) Overnight parking is not permitted at these parking areas.

The bright yellow blazes of the Beulahland Trail lead past Backpacker Campsite #1 and end at the Appalachian Trail. The trail provides an alternate route for day-hikers going to Sunfish Pond. From Old Mine Road, the trail enters an old road bed and goes gently uphill until reaching the ridgetop and the campsites. It continues on to the Appalachian Trail. From its intersection with the A.T., it is 2.2 miles to Sunfish Pond.

KARAMAC TRAIL
1.1 miles

Location: *From the Kittatinny Point Visitor Center off I-80, go north along Old Mine Road for 0.6 mile to the I-80 bridge over the Delaware River. The trail starts just north of the bridge, at a pipe gate to the left, by the traffic light. There is a small parking area here.*

This level hike along an old railroad bed leads to a bridge abutment where the railroad once crossed the river. There is a fine view of the river here. The trail is

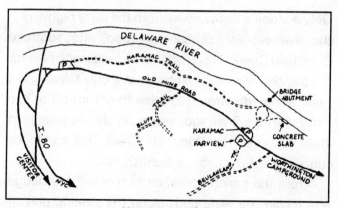

Karamac Trail

suited for a gentle hike and can also be used as a jogging path.

The trail ends at the Karamac Parking Area one mile north along Old Mine Road. Several paths lead from the parking area down to the river, where there is a slab of rock and the bridge abutment. This is a popular area for anglers.

DUNNFIELD CREEK TRAIL	*Location:* Park at *Dunnfield Creek*
3.5 miles	*Parking Area off I-80.*

Only a stone's throw away from the busy highway is the ever-popular, refreshingly cool and soothing Dunnfield Creek. This trail offers a becalming hike for the frazzled nerves. Most hikers will only take a short walk along the stream, or else they turn off at the Holly Springs Trail and return on the Appalachian Trail. However, the Dunnfield Creek Trail continues further as a faint path to Sunfish Pond.

From the parking area, cross the first footbridge and follow the wide path along the stream, part of the white-blazed Appalachian Trail. After 0.4 mile, the A.T. veers left and upwards to Sunfish Pond.

Here, the green-blazed Dunnfield Creek Trail begins. The blue-blazed Blue Dot Trail also starts here, and both trails follow a woods road upstream along Dunnfield Creek. Soon, you will cross the second footbridge. In another 300 feet, the Blue Dot Trail turns right and begins its climb to Mt. Tammany. The green-blazed Dunnfield Creek Trail continues along the stream, crossing a third and fourth footbridge and then the fifth and final footbridge. A short distance past this last footbridge (1.2 miles from the start of the trail), the Holly Springs Trail goes off to the left. Most people turn left here and follow the Holly Springs Trail 0.4 mile to the Appalachian Trail, which they take back to the start, thus completing the "Dunnfield Loop."

From here, the trail to Sunfish Pond is much fainter. Follow the creek, crossing several bridges, until you reach a grassy meadow that was a beaver swamp. Here, the faint path skirts the left side of the meadow. Follow it carefully as it slants upwards through the thick brush of a 1976 burn and finally emerges at Sunfish Pond.

HOLLY SPRINGS TRAIL
0.4 mile

This grassy roadbed connects the Appalachian Trail and the Dunnfield Creek Trail. It begins at the intersection of the A.T. and the Beulahland Trail, and descends eastward to the Dunnfield Creek Trail. Many people hike these three trails together as the "Dunnfield Loop," a three-mile jaunt. The fairly reliable Holly Spring is located halfway along the trail (water should be purified).

APPALACHIAN TRAIL: I-80 TO CAMP ROAD
8.8 miles

Location: Park at the Dunnfield Creek Parking Area across from the Kittatinny Point Visitor Center.

An extremely popular hike follows the white-blazed Appalachian Trail (A.T.) 3.7 miles from the Dunnfield Creek Parking Area to Sunfish Pond—quite a famous spot in New Jersey. Mt. Mohican, just north of Sunfish Pond, provides a panoramic view.

The section of trail to Mt. Mohican is within Worthington State Forest. Backpackers hiking the Appalachian Trail can camp at Backpacker Campsites

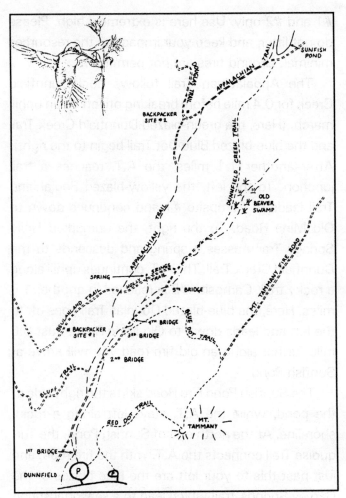

Appalachian Trail: I-80 North

#1 and #2 only. Use here is extremely high. Please do not litter, and keep your impact on the resources minimal. Ground fires are not permitted.

The Appalachian Trail follows cool Dunnfield Creek for 0.4 mile before breaking off left on an uphill march. (Here, the green-blazed Dunnfield Creek Trail and the blue-blazed Blue Dot Trail begin to the right). After another 1.1 miles, the A.T. reaches a trail junction. To the left, the yellow-blazed Beulahland Trail leads to Campsite #1 and continues down to Old Mine Road. To the right, the unmarked Holly Springs Trail passes a spring and descends to the Dunnfield Creek Trail. The A.T. continues uphill along a rocky trail. Campsite #2 is reached in another 1.6 miles. Here, the blue-blazed Douglas Trail goes off to the left and leads down to Old Mine Road. Just 0.6 mile further along an old fire road you will arrive at Sunfish Pond.

The Sunfish Pond Fire Road skirts the right side of the pond, while the A.T. stays left along a rocky shoreline. At the north end of Sunfish Pond, the Turquoise Trail connects the A.T. with the fire road, and just past this to your left are the blue blazes of the Garvey Springs Trail which lead to a seasonal spring in 500 feet (water should be purified) and continue down to Old Mine Road. The A.T. now climbs up Mt. Mohican. At 1,480 feet, the summit provides an excellent spot for taking a break and enjoying the wonderful view.

Just down from Mt. Mohican, you leave Worthington State Forest and enter the Delaware Water Gap National Recreation Area. Soon the Kaiser Trail crosses the ridge. The A.T. follows the ridge past a good view to the east over Lower Yards Creek Reservoir (private property), then goes down to the gravel Camp Road (formerly known as Mohican Road). Just before the last descent to the road, the red-blazed Coppermines Trail goes off to the left. Blue blazes along the road lead to a water faucet at the Mohican Outdoor Center.

SUNFISH POND FIRE ROAD
1.6 miles

This is a pleasant grassy roadbed along Sunfish Pond's southern shore. It begins at an intersection with the Appalachian Trail at the western end of the pond and eventually leads to the Upper Yards Creek Reservoir, but most hikers use this trail to hike around Sunfish Pond. At 0.6 mile, near the eastern end of the pond, the Turquoise Trail goes left to the Appalachian Trail, and at 0.9 mile the Turquoise Trail leaves to the right and goes to the Mt. Tammany Fire Road. The Sunfish Pond Fire Road ends at the fence surrounding the Upper Yards Creek Reservoir. Please do not trespass on Yards Creek Reservoir property.

MT. TAMMANY FIRE ROAD

3.1 miles

Location: Park at the Dunnfield Creek Parking Area off I-80. Take the Red Dot or Blue Dot Trail up to the ridge to connect with the Fire Road. An alternate starting point is the Yards Creek Picnic Area accessible from Route 94. Hike to the reservoir and turn left around it. The Mt. Tammany Fire Road is the first road to your left (the second road on the left is the Sunfish Pond Fire Road, which leads to Sunfish Pond).

This level trail along the ridge was created during the 1976 forest fire. It is blazed blue and runs north for 3.1 miles from the Blue Dot Trail on Mt. Tammany to the Turquoise Trail. From there, it continues for about another mile as an unmarked trail to the Upper Yards

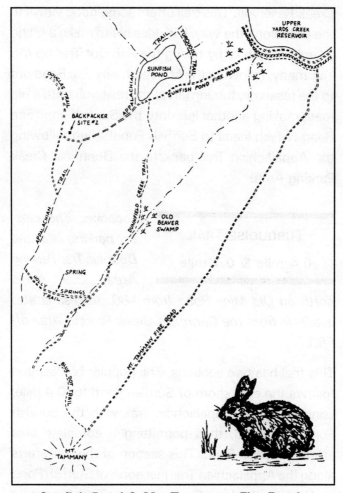

Sunfish Pond & Mt. Tammany Fire Roads

Creek Reservoir. This trail offers some good views to the east along the way. It is possible to make a grand 11-mile loop hike by taking the Red Dot Trail up Mt. Tammany, following the Mt. Tammany Fire Road out to the reservoir, turning left at the reservoir onto a fire road, making another left onto the Sunfish Pond Fire Road (which leads to Sunfish Pond), then following the Appalachian Trail back to the Dunnfield Creek Parking Area.

TURQUOISE TRAIL
0.4 mile & 0.7 mile

Location: The closest parking is at the Douglas Trail Parking Area, 3.9 miles north on Old Mine Road from I-80. Access is also available from the Dunnfield Creek Parking Area off I-80.

This trail has two sections. The popular first section follows the east shore of Sunfish Pond for 0.4 mile, connecting the Appalachian Trail with the Sunfish Pond Fire Road, thus permitting a complete hike around Sunfish Pond. This section of the trail starts along the Appalachian Trail just north of Sunfish Pond and just south of the Garvey Springs Trail. It goes up to a bluff overlooking Sunfish Pond, then proceeds across a swampy area and back up a slope to come out on the grassy fire road along the east shore of Sunfish Pond.

The second 0.7-mile section is also blazed turquoise but is more obscure. It crosses the headwaters of Dunnfield Creek (a recently burned area) and connects the Sunfish Pond Fire Road with the Mt. Tammany Fire Road.

DOUGLAS TRAIL

1.7 miles

Location: Park at the Douglas Trail Parking Area, on Old Mine Road 3.9 miles north of I-80.

The Douglas Trail is another popular route for those heading to Sunfish Pond. Its blue blazes will take you up a rough old road to the Appalachian Trail just south of Sunfish Pond. From the Douglas Trail Parking Area, cross the road and begin to follow the blue blazes. One hundred feet up the trail is a plaque commemorating former Supreme Court Justice William O. Douglas, an ardent conservationist whom the trail is named after. In 0.4 mile, the unblazed

Rockcores Trail is crossed. The Douglas Trail then narrows and, after several switchbacks, reaches the Appalachian Trail at Backpacker Site #2. From here, Sunfish Pond is 0.6 mile north along the Appalachian Trail. It is possible to combine the Douglas Trail with the Garvey Springs Trail to make a 4.3-mile loop hike up to Sunfish Pond and back.

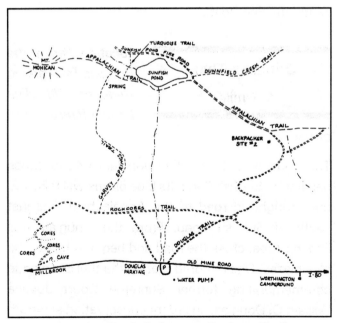

Douglas Trail & Garvey Springs Trail

GARVEY SPRINGS TRAIL

1.2 miles

Location: Park at the Douglas Trail Parking Area, 3.9 miles north on Old Mine Road from I-80.

This blue-blazed trail leads from Old Mine Road, starting about 500 feet north of the Douglas Trail Parking Area, to the Garvey Spring, a seasonal spring off the Appalachian Trail, located just north of Sunfish Pond. (Drinking water should be purified.) This trail can be combined with the Douglas Trail to make a loop hike.

From Old Mine Road, the Garvey Springs Trail follows a rough old woods road on the left side of the Sunfish Pond drainage as it slants up away from the stream. It meets the Rockcores Trail's grassy roadbed and follows it left for about 700 feet. Then the trail turns left and continues upward on a footpath to Garvey Spring. From the spring, blue blazes lead in 500 feet to the Appalachian Trail. (To reach Sunfish Pond, turn right on the Appalachian Trail for another 500 feet.)

**ROCKCORES
(NORTHWEST) TRAIL**

2.7 miles

Location: Park at a small pulloff area on the west side of Old Mine Road, 3.0 miles north of I-80.

The Rockcores Trail (formerly known as the Northwest Trail) is an old woods road which begins on the east side of Old Mine Road, ascends the ridge and parallels it at about the 900-foot elevation, and then descends back to Old Mine Road. The Rockcores Trail can also be accessed via the Douglas Trail and the Garvey Springs Trail.

From Old Mine Road, ascend moderately and then more gradually on the old woods road. In 0.7 mile, the blue-blazed Douglas Trail crosses, and at 1.4 miles from the beginning, the Garvey Springs Trail joins for about 500 feet.

To explore the northern part of the Rockcores Trail, take the Garvey Springs Trail from Old Mine Road to the Rockcores Trail, and follow the trail to the northeast as it starts to head downhill and branch off into spur roads. Scattered throughout this area are large rock core samples taken from deep within the earth during test drillings for the proposed Tocks

Island Dam. It is quite impressive to see columns of subterranean bedrock now resting in the forest exposed to the light and life. Continue downhill along the most obvious roadbed and you will come out on Old Mine Road at a cable close to the southern tip of Tocks Island. This is where the dam would have been located. Near this site is also a bored cave with fresh cold water flowing from its mouth. *The ceiling in this cave is unstable, and the entrance is fenced off for safety reasons. STAY OUT!! Do not venture past the mouth, even if vandals have opened the entrance.*

COPPERMINES TRAIL

2 miles

Location: Park at the Coppermines Trail Parking Area, on the left side of Old Mine Road, 7.8 miles north of I-80.

The Coppermines Trail is named after the old mines located along the lower portion of the trail. Although the mines are closed at the present time, this red-blazed trail is well worth hiking in its own right. The trail continues beyond the mines up to the ridge, and ends at the Appalachian Trail just south of Camp Road (formerly known as Mohican Road).

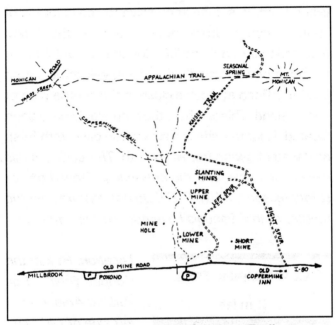

Coppermines Trail & Kaiser Trail

The Coppermines Trail begins on the east side of the road. Follow the signs to reach the lower mine, a pleasant hike of about 100 yards. To reach the upper mine, backtrack to the sign which marks the beginning of the trail. Follow the trail as it curves uphill along the steep right side of the ravine to the upper mine, which is directly alongside the trail.

Beyond the upper mine, the trail crosses the stream on a footbridge and curves uphill along the left bank. It soon passes a side trail on the right (blazed blue) which leads to the Kaiser Trail and then continues for another mile to end at the Appalachian Trail just south of Camp Road. (There are also several other lesser mine holes in the area. Refer to the map if you wish to scout them out.)

Two loop hikes are possible using the Coppermines Trail. A short two-mile loop would follow the Coppermines Trail for one mile, turn right and take the blue-blazed side trail to the Kaiser Trail, then turn right again on the Kaiser Trail and follow it back to the start. To return to the start, make sure you take the right fork of the Kaiser Trail when it branches.

A second longer but very interesting six-mile loop would be to take the Coppermines Trail up to the white-blazed Appalachian Trail, turn right and follow the Appalachian Trail south almost two miles to the Kaiser Trail, then turn right and take the Kaiser Trail back down to the start. Before heading back down the Kaiser Trail, you may wish to continue a bit further along the Appalachian Trail to the top of Mt. Mohican for a rewarding view to the west over the wide river valley.

KAISER TRAIL

2 miles (to A.T.)

Location: *Park at the Coppermines Trail Parking Area, on the left side of Old Mine Road, 7.8 miles north of I-80. (Another spur starts across from the Old Coppermine Inn.)*

The Kaiser Trail is an old grassy roadbed with two branches, one of which starts at the Coppermines Trail Parking Area, and one of which starts at the Old Coppermine Inn. Both merge into one trail, which makes a sharp turn as it slants up the ridge to join the Appalachian Trail for a short distance at the top of the ridge. Just before the summit of Mt. Mohican (also known as Raccoon Ridge), the trail drops down the east side of the ridge and leads to the Lower Yards Creek Reservoir.

The Kaiser Trail, together with the Coppermines Trail, can be used to make two loop hikes. (Refer to the Coppermines Trail description.)

**VAN CAMPENS
GLEN TRAIL**

¼ mile

Location: From the Visitor Center along I-80, follow Old Mine Road north 10.5 miles to the Lower Glen Picnic Area, which is on the right, just past the Depew Picnic Area. The Upper Glen Parking Area is one mile past this (11.5 miles from I-80) and on the left. (The Watergate Picnic Area is 1.3 miles north of the Upper Glen. You may also park at Watergate and follow an old road along the east side of the stream to the Upper Glen.)

Van Campens Brook flows from Blue Mountain Lakes and Long Pond past Millbrook Village and through the Watergate Picnic Area. It then passes through "The Glen" and finally meets the Delaware River by Poxono Island. The area known as "The Glen" is between the Upper Glen Parking Area and the Lower Glen Picnic Area, which is a distance of one mile.

It is always refreshingly cool in the Glen. The stream is picturesque, and there are two small waterfalls with pools below them. The trails at each end are well defined, leading to the upper and lower falls. The middle section has no trail, and because of

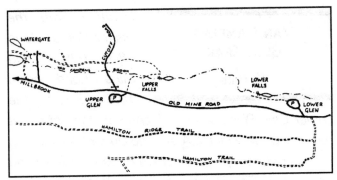

Van Campens Glen Trail

erosion and unsafe conditions you should not hike in this area.

Van Campens Brook is a native trout stream. Special regulations apply for fishing. Two other special regulations are posted and enforced in the Glen Area: No alcoholic beverages are allowed, and diving is not permitted in the pools of the stream (due to serious injuries that have occurred here).

To approach The Glen from the Upper Glen Parking Area, follow the closed-off paved road that starts across from the parking area. Continue along the road a bit beyond the small bridge and up to a path leading to the right. The path extends along the opposite side of the stream to the upper falls and pool.

The Lower Glen Picnic Area is small, but it provides a quiet spot for a sunny afternoon picnic. A short hike up The Glen is a nice way to work off a picnic lunch. The trail follows the stream a short distance to the lower falls and pool. This set of falls is somewhat smaller than the upper falls, but it still provides a cool, refreshing atmosphere on the hottest of summer days.

RATTLESNAKE SWAMP TRAIL

2½ miles

Location: Follow Route 602 to the crest of the ridge 1.2 miles east of Millbrook, and park next to the pipe gate (do not block the gate).

If you are expecting a rattlesnake-infested swamp you may be disappointed. This interesting two-and-one-half-mile trail is swampy only after rainstorms, and you should count yourself lucky (?) if you see just one rattlesnake. The trail is blazed orange and leads two miles to Catfish Pond. It then turns uphill for half a mile to meet the Appalachian Trail. Done as a loop with the Appalachian Trail, it makes an excellent 4.5-mile day hike.

Follow the fire road and the Appalachian Trail for 0.4 mile to Rattlesnake Spring (water should be purified), where the Appalachian Trail goes off to the left. Orange blazes start here and follow the fire road for a short distance to a trail sign, where the orange blazes veer right along a trail. The Rattlesnake Swamp Trail follows a shallow valley along the edge of swampy terrain and is generally level out to Catfish Pond.

At Catfish Pond, the trail curves up an old road close to the perimeter of the Mohican Outdoor Center, and then goes steeply up for ¼ mile to join the Appalachian Trail. If you turn left (north) on the Appalachian Trail, it will lead you past the Catfish Fire Tower to and back to Rattlesnake Spring, where you started your "rattlesnake" adventure.

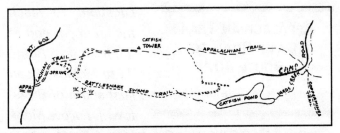

Rattlesnake Swamp Trail & Appalachian Trail

CATFISH FIRE TOWER ROAD

1¼ mile

Location: Follow Route 602 to the crest of the ridge, 1.2 miles east of Millbrook, and park next to the pipe gate (do not block the gate).

From the gate, the fire road leads over a mile to the Catfish Fire Tower, a fire lookout point used during the spring and fall fire seasons. A panorama from the ridge top is the main attraction here. The Appalachian Trail and Rattlesnake Swamp Trail both follow this road for some distance, but they then branch off and separate, following their white and orange blazes. Rattlesnake Spring is a reliable spring along the road on the way to the tower (water should be purified).

APPALACHIAN TRAIL: CAMP ROAD TO ROUTE 602

3.3 miles

Location: To reach the southern end of the hike, take Route 94 to Mohican Road (just south of Blairstown). Follow Mohican Road for 3.5 miles to Gaisler Road, turn left onto Gaisler Road, then take the next right onto Camp Road, which leads to the A.T. crossing, where limited parking is available (do not block the gates).

If you are heading north from Camp Road, the Appalachian Trail quickly gains the ridge and follows it past some nice views looking east. It passes the end of the Rattlesnake Swamp Trail and continues on to the Catfish Fire Tower. The fairly reliable Rattlesnake Spring is 0.6 mile beyond the tower (water should be purified). From the spring, the A.T. follows a gravel road out to Millbrook-Blairstown Road (Route 602).

From Route 602, you can do a two-mile (round-trip) hike by following the A.T. to the fire tower and returning the same way. For a more interesting 4.5-mile loop, follow the A.T. past the fire tower one more mile to the orange-blazed Rattlesnake Swamp Trail; follow it past Catfish Pond and back to your car.

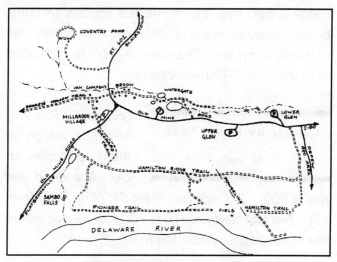

Millbrook-Watergate Trail

| MILLBROOK-WATERGATE TRAIL 1 mile | *Location:* Park at Millbrook Village, at the intersection of Old Mine Road and Route 602, 12.3 |

miles north on Old Mine Road from I-80.

This pleasant, one-mile stroll along Van Campens Brook connects Millbrook Village with the Watergate Picnic Area. For its entire length, the trail follows an old road. If you walk quietly along the trail in the early evening, you may see numerous species of birds, beaver, deer, rabbits, and other mammals in this area of marsh and ponds. The walk may also be combined with a tour of Millbrook Village.

COVENTRY POND TRAIL
½ mile

Location: Park at Millbrook Village, at the intersection of Old Mine Road and Route 602, 12.3 miles north on Old Mine Road from I-80. The trail starts at a gate 100 feet east of where the brook passes under the road.

From the gate, an old road leads one-half mile to Coventry Pond, where the beaver have built a lodge. A path circles the pond for easy view of the entire area. This trail provides an excellent opportunity for a quiet hike while in Millbrook.

DONKEY'S HOLLOW TRAIL

**2 miles or
4 miles entire**

Location: Park at Millbrook Village.

An easy walk along a pleasant stream and through beautiful quiet woods, this trail begins at Millbrook Village and continues north along the west side of the Van Campens Brook. A short two-mile walk on this trail will bring you out at Donkey's Corners on Route 624. The Donkey's Hollow Trail continues beyond Donkey's Corners for another two miles to Mountain Road.

HAMILTON RIDGE TRAIL

2½ miles

Location: The trailhead is 0.7 mile north of Millbrook Village along Old Mine Road. Park by the pipe gate near Sambo Pond. You can also park at Millbrook Village and take the Orchard Trail to intersect the Hamilton Ridge Trail.

The Hamilton Ridge Trail is an old, partially paved road along forested Hamilton Ridge. It is a pleasant walk with a level grade, and is suited for wheelchairs for a short distance. A casual stroll along this ''paved trail'' will often be rewarded with a sighting of deer or wild turkeys.

ORCHARD TRAIL & PIONEER TRAIL
¼ mile & 5 miles

Location: *Park at Millbrook Village, with the trail starting across the road from the parking area.*

The Orchard Trail is an old road leading to the Hamilton Ridge Trail. It starts by a berm along a faint roadbed, then passes a little spring and continues through a clearing and on to the Hamilton Ridge Trail.

The Pioneer Trail is a longer loop hike of 5 miles which explores the slides of Sambo Falls and an intriguing old road along the Delaware River before returning. To start, take the Orchard Trail to the Hamilton Ridge Trail, and turn right on it for a short way. An old road leading left (west) with green blazes marks the beginning of this trail. Follow the blazes downhill. The road turns into a rugged path leading steeply down to Sambo Falls near the river. Here the blazes follow a hand-laid road believed by some to be the original Old Mine Road. Follow this for two miles along the river until the green blazes lead left, past cedars, along a stone wall and up to another old road, and finally to the Hamilton Ridge Trail. Turn left, back to the Orchard Trail, then go right on the Orchard Trail to return to Millbrook Village.

APPALACHIAN TRAIL: RTE 602 TO RTE 624
3.8 miles

Location: To reach the southern end of the hike, follow Route 602 to the crest of the ridge 1.2 miles east of Millbrook, and park next to the pipe gate. Or, if you wish to start from the north, take Route 602 to Route 624, and continue to the Trail crossing, where parking is available.

From Route 602, the white-blazed Appalachian Trail heads north past small Black Pond and up to the ridge crest, where it reaches a powerline with a good view east. It then weaves along the ridgetop. At 2.2 miles, the Trail starts following a dirt road past grassy openings—locations of former homesites—with fine views. This road leads to Route 624, which it reaches 3.8 miles from the start. There is a hand pump for water here.

**MOUNTAIN RIDGE
LAKE TRAILS
(POOL COLONY)**

½ mile & 3 miles

Location: From Route 80 at the Delaware Water Gap, follow Old Mine Road north. Continue past Mill-brook Village for 1.6 miles, and turn right on Route 624. Follow Route 624 for 1.5 miles to the Blue Mountain Lakes Parking Area (marked by a sign on the left), and continue for another 0.3 mile to a pipe gate to the right. Limited parking is available here, but you may choose to park at the larger Blue Mountain Lakes Parking Area and walk back along the road.

This area is a maze of old development roads surrounding a partially washed-out Mountain Ridge Lake. The pattern of the roads is not easy to discern, and it is therefore recommended that only experienced hikers, with a good sense of direction, attempt to hike in this area. To reach the lake from the pipe gate, turn right and follow the road for one mile, then take the second left to the lake. If you carefully consult the map you can follow an old road around the lake and explore other roads.

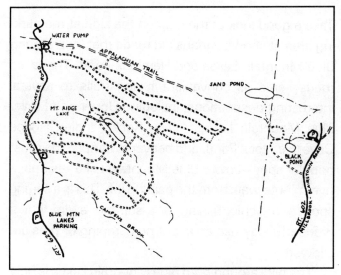

Mountain Ridge Lake Trails

BLUE MOUNTAIN LAKES TRAILS

¼ miles, 2 miles or 5 miles

Location: From Route 80 at the Delaware Water Gap, follow Old Mine Road north. Continue past Millbrook Village for 1.6 miles, and turn right on Route 624. Follow Route 624 for 1.5 miles to the Blue Mountain Lakes Parking Area (marked by a sign on the left).

Take a good look at the map on the sign at the parking area. It shows various old roads that loop around Blue Mountain Lakes and Hemlock Pond. These old roads serve as convenient hiking trails to several interesting destinations, including Upper and Lower Blue Mountain Lakes, Indian Rocks, Indian House Cave, Hemlock Pond, and beaver swamps. The most popular spot—Lower Blue Mountain Lake—is only a five-minute walk from the parking lot. This is a serene spot for a picnic, fishing, or a summer swim. It is a wonderful day-use area, but no camping or fires are allowed.

The hike around both Blue Mountain Lakes is only two miles long. You can also take a side trail up to Indian Rocks, which is a craggy viewpoint looking over the Wallpack Valley and into Pennsylvania. A green-blazed path from Indian Rocks leads a short way to Indian House Cave. This is a small fault (fracture) cave, and is nothing at all like the more typical limestone caves elsewhere.

Hemlock Pond is two miles from the parking area. The scenic hemlocks surrounding the pond give it the wild beauty typical of more northern latitudes. Near Hemlock Pond are recent beaver swamps. Beavers

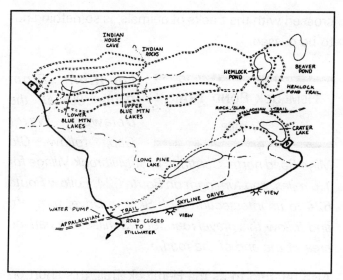

Blue Mountain Lakes Trails

are well established in this area. You may also see
black bear skat, indicating the presence of black
bears, which find this area rather homey. On the east
shore of Hemlock Pond is the orange-blazed Hemlock
Pond Trail, which leads for about one-quarter mile to
the Appalachian Trail overlooking Crater Lake.

During wintertime, the old roads here offer perhaps the best cross-country skiing in New Jersey.
The trails are well maintained for skiing. The exhilara-
tion of gliding through the magic white forest, criss-

crossed with the tracks of animals, is something not to be missed.

HEMLOCK POND TRAIL

¼ mile

Location: From Route 80 at the Delaware Water Gap, follow Old Mine Road north. Continue past Millbrook Village for 1.6 miles, and turn right on Route 624. Follow Route 624 to its intersection with Skyline Drive, turn left, and follow this gravel road for 2.3 miles to a parking area at the end of the road.

Also referred to as the Hemlock Trail, this short orange-blazed trail leads from the bluff at Crater Lake, on the Appalachian Trail, to the more secretive Hemlock Pond. To reach the beginning of this trail, hike around the Crater Lake Loop Road to the right as it circles the lake. This road meets the white-blazed Appalachian Trail along the bluff. Turn right (north) and in 100 feet you will see the sign and orange blazes of the Hemlock Pond Trail.

Follow the Hemlock Pond Trail down to Hemlock Pond's east shore. You can circle Hemlock Pond, using the old road system. Or, if you are interested in a longer five-mile hike, go around the pond and north to the beaver swamp. Cross the swamp on the dam and continue along the Woods Road Trail for one mile until you intersect the blue-blazed Buttermilk Falls Trail. Turn right and follow this trail uphill to the ridge, where it meets the white-blazed Appalachian Trail. Turn right on the Appalachian Trail and follow it back to Crater Lake.

CRATER LAKE TRAIL
7 miles

Location: From Route 80 at the Delaware Water Gap, follow Old Mine Road north. Continue past Millbrook Village for 1.6 miles, and turn right on Route 624. Follow Route 624 to its intersection with Skyline Drive, and park here. The trail starts by the garbage cans.

Begin by following the old road east of Skyline Drive, then take a path across to roads west of Skyline Drive. The trail passes close to Crater Lake. Continue uphill to the bluff, where you intersect the Appalachian Trail. If you wish, you can turn left on the Appalachian Trail and follow it back to Route 624 and Skyline Drive.

CRATER LAKE LOOP HIKE
2 miles

Location: From Route 80 at the Delaware Water Gap, follow Old Mine Road north. Continue past Millbrook Village for 1.6 miles, and turn right on Route 624. Follow Route 624 to its intersection with Skyline Drive, turn left, and follow this gravel road for 2.3 miles to a parking area at the end of the road.

Crater Lake—an attractive natural lake high atop the Kittatinny Ridge—may have been formed by the impact of a large meteor in 1853. The crater soon filled with rain water. A two-mile trail, consisting of old roads, leads around the lake. There is a view on the far side where the Appalachian Trail follows an old road along the bluff. You may also use the Crater Lake loop road as a start for a hike to Hemlock Pond via the Hemlock Pond Trail. Or go left around Crater Lake and at the elbow bend take a blazed path leading either to Long Pine Pond or out to a rock slab. Other options are possible—just consult the map.

Note: *Only A.T. thru-hikers may camp on the Trail, and no camping is permitted on the bluff across the lake. The Crater Lake area is closed 10 P.M. to 6 A.M.*

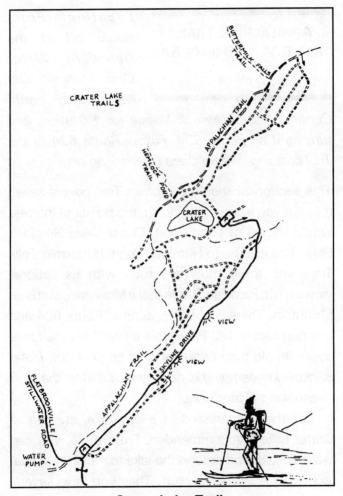

Crater Lake Trails

**APPALACHIAN TRAIL:
RTE 624 TO BRINKS RD**

7 miles

Location: From Route 80 at the Delaware Water Gap, follow Old Mine Road north. Continue past Millbrook Village for 1.6 miles, and turn right on Route 624. Follow Route 624 to the Trail crossing, where there is a parking area.

This section of the Appalachian Trail covers seven miles. If you are heading north, the points of interest would be: tip of Long Pond, Crater Lake, Hemlock Pond Trail leading to Hemlock Pond, Buttermilk Falls Trail, and three mountain tops with exceptional views—Mt. Paradise, Rattlesnake Mountain, and Blue Mountain. There is a water pump at Route 624 and a spring east of Mt. Paradise's summit one-half mile down an old road (water should be purified). *Note: Backpacker camping is not permitted atop the bluff overlooking Crater Lake.*

For those interested in a day hike, starting at Crater Lake is recommended. From there, you can walk the old road around the lake to meet the Appalachian Trail along the bluff. Then you have several different options: Take the Hemlock Pond Trail to

Hemlock Pond, a very pretty spot, head north to the Buttermilk Falls Trail (quite a hike if you go down to the falls), go further north to see the view from Mt. Paradise, or head south and continue along the blazed path leading to Long Pine Pond's old beach.

WOODS ROAD TRAIL

4 miles

Location: This trail may be most easily accessed from Crater Lake, Buttermilk Falls or Brinks Road east of Walpack Center. There is also access from Blue Mountain Lakes.

The Woods Road Trail is an old forest road which heads north from Hemlock Pond, passes two beaver swamps, and goes up Rattlesnake Mountain, where it merges with the Appalachian Trail. It then continues downhill to Brinks Road above Tillmans Ravine in Stokes State Forest. The Woods Road Trail may be followed in conjunction with the Appalachian Trail or the Buttermilk Falls Trail to make a good day's loop hike. Scan the map for possibilities.

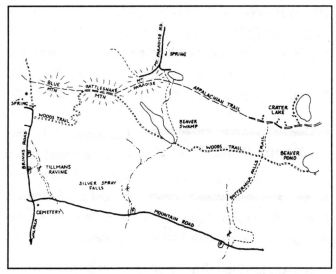

Woods Road Trail & Buttermilk Falls Trail

BUTTERMILK FALLS TRAIL	*Location:* From
1.9 miles	*Walpack Center (by the former Post Office), go east for*

half a mile, then turn south (at the cemetery) along Mountain Road. Continue along Mountain Road for about two miles until you see Buttermilk Falls on the left. Parking is available on the west side of the road.

Buttermilk Falls is a picturesque waterfall right by the road. It gains or loses character depending on the

amount of water cascading over it. The blue-on-white-blazed Buttermilk Falls Trail climbs for 1.9 miles to the Appalachian Trail on the ridge.

From the waterfall, the trail goes south along the road for a short distance, then turns left and climbs around to the top of the falls. (Do not climb directly along the falls.) The trail continues uphill, crossing the Woods Road Trail, and ends at the Appalachian Trail, 1.2 miles north of Crater Lake.

For a suggested loop hike: Start at the Buttermilk Falls Trail, and follow it to Woods Road. Turn right on Woods Road for one mile to the beaver dam, and continue past it to Hemlock Pond. Follow the road around Hemlock Pond to the orange blazes of the

Hemlock Pond Trail. Take the Hemlock Pond Trail uphill for one-quarter mile until it meets the Appalachian Trail (by Crater Lake). Follow the white-blazed Appalachian Trail north for one-and-one-quarter miles to the top of the Buttermilk Falls Trail, which may then be followed back to the parking area. This is a nice round trip of six and one-half miles.

TILLMANS RAVINE TRAIL
1 mile

Location: From Walpack Center (by the former Post Office), proceed east for half a mile to an intersection by the cemetery. Continue straight ahead at the intersection into Stokes State Forest. Just up the hill are two pull-off areas to park.

This enjoyable trail takes you along a cool stream that cuts through a hemlock-lined ravine. This soothing little hike is actually in Stokes State Forest, just outside the boundary of the Delaware Water Gap National Recreation Area. Check out the other trails available at Stokes State Forest by visiting their office along Route 206.

THUNDER MOUNTAIN TRAIL

2 miles

Location: You can start either at the southern end of the trail (park at the former Walpack Center Post Office), or at the northern end (from Peters Valley, follow signs to Thunder Mountain, and park by the lake).

This trail through lush vegetation and around a huge beaver pond makes a splendid two-mile round trip. If you start at Walpack, proceed west on the old road

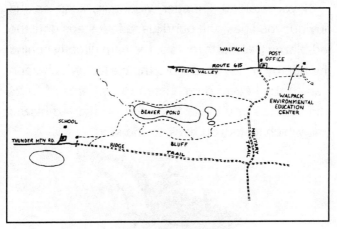

Thunder Mountain Trail

across from the Post Office. Stay on it until you see a pond off to your right. A path will soon lead you right to the very edge of this soupy pond. Now start following cherry red blazes along a path leading up and along a bluff. Soon you'll be looking down on a surprisingly large swamp-pond. Keep following the blazes, as they drop down to the pond's edge. Cross planks and continue along a grassy path to the beaver dam, cross the footbridge to the other shore, then go up and away from the pond. If you stay on the path through some thick vegetation, you will emerge back on the road close to where you started.

If you start at Thunder Mountain, keep on the obvious road past the pond just a few steps until the red-blazed trail starts (or take the path directly behind the nearby building). Follow the blazes, which soon lead to the beaver dam. Listen to a chorus of frogs and birds as you circle the pond on the red-blazed trail which leads you back to the start.

YOUTH HOSTEL TRAILS

1 mile to 7 miles entire

Location: Park at the pull-offs near the entrance to the American Youth Hostel, along Old Mine Road approximately two and one half miles north of the Dingmans Ferry Bridge.

The American Youth Hostel maintains a network of trails that are primarily used for cross-country skiing in the winter. These trails are marked, and a map is available at the hostel. The skiing is quite diverse, with trails both along the river and atop the ridge.

Some of the trails are good for hiking, the most popular spot being around Camp Kittatinny, located

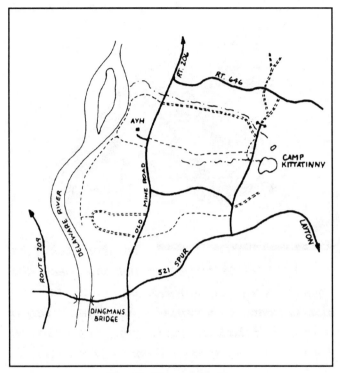

Youth Hostel Trails

on a small pond along a ridgetop. An old road follows the rather open ridgeline north of Camp Kittatinny. Walking along this section affords some pretty views across the fields and thickets.

PENNSYLVANIA

TRAILS

PENNSYLVANIA TRAILS

**APPALACHIAN TRAIL:
MT. MINSI**

5 miles (round trip)

Location: The trailhead is off Route 611 in the village of Delaware Water Gap, Pa. The main parking area is at Lake Lenape. Turn off Route 611 at the Deer Head Inn (a right turn traveling south, or a left turn traveling north) and then turn left into the Lake Lenape Parking Area. You can also park at Resort Point Overlook (on the east side of Route 611, about ½ mile south of the village of Delaware Water Gap, Pa.). From the overlook, carefully cross Route 611 and take a side trail up to meet the A.T.

This is a popular hike up the other great gatepost of The Gap, Mt. Minsi. Follow the white blazes along the fire road past Lake Lenape. Soon the fire road branches right, while the Appalachian Trail stays on a gradual incline close to the mountain's edge. It crosses a stream, the outlet of Lake Latini, and reaches a rocky prow with a good view down to the Delaware River and Mt. Tammany.

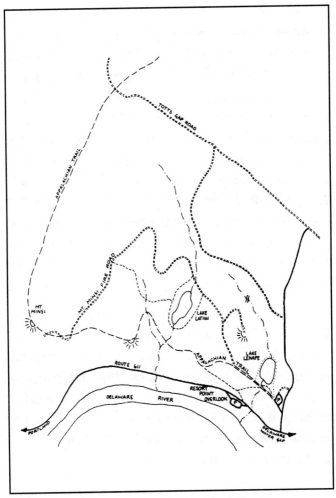

Appalachian Trail: Mt. Minsi

You are over half way to Mt. Minsi, but the trail now gets steeper. After crossing the end of the Mt. Minsi Fire Road (you may want to follow the fire road on your way down to make a loop hike), the trail comes out at Lookout Rock, another fine viewpoint looking way down to The Gap. The summit (1,461 feet) is only about a quarter of a mile further. From the summit, the trail follows a fire road west along the ridgetop to a microwave tower at Totts Gap, another two miles away.

The most scenic spots along this section of the Trail are Lake Lenape and the two rocky viewpoints. The actual summit affords no view, but it is "the top," so it is popular. Mt. Minsi is a popular hike; please do not litter along this heavily used trail.

MT. MINSI FIRE ROAD **1½ mile**	***Location:*** *Follow directions to the Mt. Minsi/Appalachian Trail hike, above.*

The Mt. Minsi Fire Road branches off the Appalachian Trail after Lake Lenape. Soon another road leads right, for a short distance, to a grassy bluff with a fine view of The Gap. Continue on the fire road further uphill, past another side road to your left, until the fire road rejoins the Appalachian Trail, just before a rocky viewpoint.

For a loop hike up Mt. Minsi, it is probably preferable to take the Appalachian Trail up, and follow the Mt. Minsi Fire Road back down. There are several side roads around Lake Latini, but if you stay on the most obvious one (the fire road) you will return straight to the parking area.

SLATEFORD SKI TRAILS

various mileages

Location: From the village of Delaware Water Gap, Pa., on the west side of the I-80 bridge over the Delaware River, take Route 611 south to National Park Drive. Turn right and go 1.2 miles to a pull-off on the right by a duck pond.

There are several hikes in the Slateford area (see map on page 59). One popular destination is an abandoned quarry, now a deep crater filled with turquoise water. A short trail leads to its edge. Many people walk around the restored Slateford Farm in the summer, and in the winter the trails are marked for cross-country skiing (see below). The Arrow Island

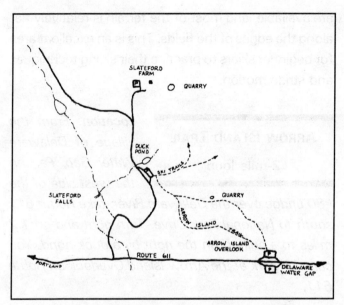

Slateford Trails & Arrow Island Trail

Trail connects the Slateford area with Arrow Island Overlook on Route 611.

SLATEFORD SKI TRAILS **5½ miles entire**	*Location: Follow the Slateford Trails directions, above.*

Bulletin boards in the parking area show the ski trails, and a map box is located a few feet in along the trail. Several ski loops are available, and most of the terrain is relatively flat along the edges of the fields. This is an excellent area for beginner skiers to practice their skiing techniques and stride motion.

ARROW ISLAND TRAIL
2-mile loop

Location: From the village of Delaware Water Gap, Pa., on the west side of the I-80 bridge over the Delaware River, take Route 611 south to National Park Drive. Turn right and go 1.2 miles to a pull-off on the right by a duck pond. You can also park at the Arrow Island Overlook on Route 611.

This blue-blazed trail follows old roads out to a view above Arrow Island, then passes a small quarry before looping back to the Slateford parking area.

HIDDEN LAKE TRAIL
1½ miles

Location: Just south of Bushkill along Route 209 (at Fernwood Resort), turn off east at the sign for National Park Service Headquarters. Follow this road three quarters of a mile, and turn right at the sign for Hidden Lake. Hidden Lake beach and picnic area are approximately two miles down the road from the right turn.

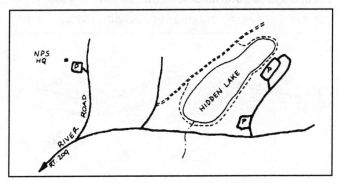

Hidden Lake Trail

This 1½-mile path circles Hidden Lake, following close to the shore all the way. Near the old lodge, the path tends to meander, so follow the lake shore to regain the trail. The hike is a pleasant way to work up an appetite for lunch. Don't forget your fishing gear!

HOGSBACK TRAILS

½ mile to 2 miles

Location: At Bushkill along Route 209, just south of the blinking light and before the red brick church, is a road to a parking area. Follow this dirt road for a short distance, then park before the road starts to go uphill.

The Hogsback is a ridge overlooking the Delaware River. The resistant rock strata of the Hogsback has forced the river to make a very obvious "river bend."

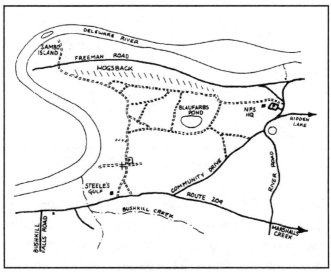

Hogsback Trails

From where you park, you can continue following the road as it climbs the Hogsback to overlook the Delaware River, with New Jersey in the background. If you wish to go down to the river, keep following the road as it descends the point of the ridge, coming out on dirt Freeman Road (driveable). Continue straight ahead at this intersection, following a dirt lane across the flats to the river by Sambo Island. You may want to relax here and watch the canoes running the Sambo-Mary rapids before heading back.

Another nice hike is to follow the road as it heads uphill but take the first road branching right. This will lead you shortly to Blaufarbs Pond, a quiet little spot to sit for a while. If you continue past the pond and veer left at the next fork in the road, you come out at the crest of the Hogsback by a power line. Then you can follow the Hogsback all the way back to the point where the first road leads you back to your car.

Anglers may want to go left from the parking spot to meet Bushkill Creek before it enters the Delaware.

BUSHKILL FALLS TRAIL
½ mile to 1½ miles

Location: From Bushkill, turn west at the blinking traffic light. Continue several miles to the marked entrance gate of the falls complex.

The largest falls and biggest attraction in the area, it is privately operated and just outside the National Recreation Area boundary. Well-built trails lead in a zig-zag fashion over bridges and steps, and past magnificent views of falls and cascades, through this picturesque gorge. Refreshments and curio shops are available, along with other features.

REVERY POND TRAIL
¼ mile

Location: Park on the dirt road intersecting Route 209 at the milepost 4 marker, located 2.5 miles north of Bushkill.

This is a short hike to a nice-sized pond, a place to spend an hour or two with nature. You can follow the old road with a bend to the pond or else take a more direct path straight to it.

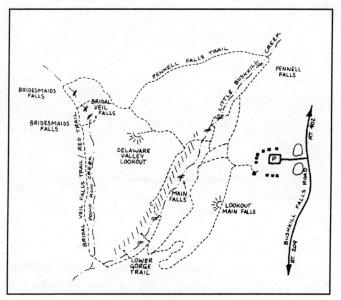

Bushkill Falls Trail

TOMS CREEK TRAIL
½ mile to 1 mile

Location: Follow Route 209 north from the Bushkill light for 3 miles, turn left by the sign onto Egypt Mills Road, and follow it a short distance to the Toms Creek Picnic Area and parking.

From the small picnic area, an old road runs alongside Toms Creek—there are no waterfalls, but there are

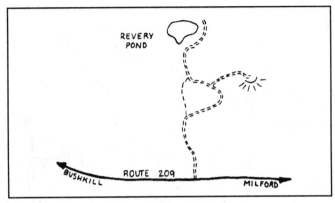

REVERY
POND

ROUTE 209

BUSHKILL   MILFORD

Revery Pond Trail

many small dams. For a short hike, you can walk
along this road, listening to the stream's babble.
Eventually the trail starts criss-crossing the stream.
You should turn around here unless you would like to
get your feet wet. If so, by all means take your shoes
off, put your toes in the cold water, hobble across
the rough slippery stream bed . . . and continue.

TOMS TRAIL TO EGYPT

1 mile

*Location: Follow
directions to Toms
Creek Trail (above).*

There are no pyra-
mids along this route; rather, it is a trail from Toms

Creek up to Egypt Mills Pond. Follow the Toms Creek Trail for a little over half a mile. Just a bit after a short downhill section, look for a trail (old road) to the right that is not really obvious at the start. After a twist, it crosses a streamlet and continues on up to Egypt Mills Pond. For a loop hike, you can follow the road back downhill to the Toms Creek Picnic Area.

POCONO RIM TRAIL
4 to 6 miles

Location: Follow Route 209 north from the Bushkill light for 4.5 miles (or go 1.9 miles south from Brisco Mountain Road), and park in the Eshback Access Parking Area. (Parking at the trailhead is not recommended, due to limited visibility in exiting and entering Route 209.)

This beautiful hike follows the rim of the Pocono plateau. From the parking area, walk back up the Eshback Access Road and carefully cross Route 209. On the opposite side of the road, near the white barns, find the old road that slants upwards (west) to the rim. After a twist, you will reach the top of the rim at a fork in the road. Take the left fork, and continue gradually uphill along the rim, until the road

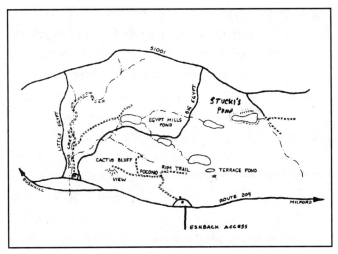

Pocono Rim Trail & Stucki's Pond

ends off the east edge of the rim. A few steps ahead is a bluff with cactus—an open grassy clearing with a clear view of the Kittatinny Ridge. Be careful not to sit down on a cactus!

STUCKI'S POND

½ mile

Location: Follow Route 209 north from the Bushkill light for 3 miles, and turn left on Egypt Mills Road. Continue on Egypt Mills Road for about ¼ mile, and make the first left onto *paved Big Egypt Road. Follow Big Egypt Road to its intersection with Milford Road. Turn right (north) here and go precisely 0.3 mile. Turn right on the dirt road, and travel less than a mile to Stucki's Pond on your right.*

Stucki's Pond is a rather out-of-the-way spot. It is a fairly long lake and provides some good fishing opportunities. You can hike around it by following a small path along the east shore. The path disappears at the far end, but if you slant up the bluff along the west shore and follow along the crest looking down on the lake it will lead you back to the road.

Pocono Environmental Education Center (PEEC)

various mileages

Location: Follow Route 209 north to Brisco Mountain Road, which is 7 miles north of Bushkill and 6 miles south of Dingmans Ferry. Follow Brisco Mountain Road up the steep hill until you arrive at PEEC. Parking is available in the lot by the office, and trail maps may be obtained in the office.

The Pocono Environmental Education Center offers a variety of nature programs as a resident environmental education facility. Check at the office for a schedule of their programs. PEEC has several blazed hiking trails, described below.

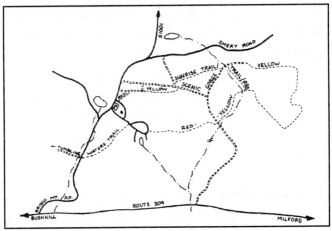

Pocono Environmental Education Center

Sunrise Trail (5 miles). From the north end of the PEEC parking lot, this yellow-blazed trail will take you through the forest on a five-mile hike. This is a pretty trail that is long but not really tiring.

Scenic Gorge Trail (2 miles). This red-blazed trail begins by running jointly with the Sunrise Trail. It follows trails and old roads to and along Spackmans Creek as it flows through a small hemlock gorge, and then goes back to PEEC. It is an easy two-mile hike, but it requires hopping over the stream at two points.

Fossil Trail (½ mile). From the parking lot, go back along the road leading into PEEC until you see the blue-blazed Fossil Trail leading off to the right (together with the orange-blazed Tumbling Waters Trail). The trail goes down steeply to a small stream and a rock outcrop where marine fossils have been found. It then returns uphill to PEEC. Please, if you do find any fossils, leave them for others to enjoy. It is a federal offense to remove them from the Park.

TUMBLING WATERS TRAIL
3 miles

Location: From the parking lot, go back along the road leading into the PEEC until you see the orange blazes for the Tumbling Waters Trail (near cabin #11).

This fine scenic trail with a touch of adventure leads past some fine views before a side branch descends into a hemlock ravine. Continue along the orange blazes that lead you uphill to a stand of tall pines and past Pickerel Pond to the parking lot.

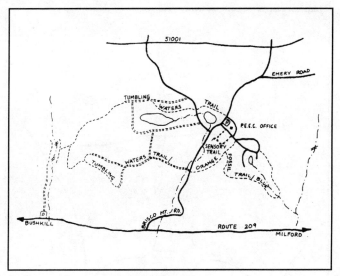

Tumbling Waters Trail

DINGMANS FALLS TRAIL	*Location:* From
½ mile or 1½ miles	*Route 209 south of*

Location: From Route 209 south of the Dingmans Ferry light, take Johnny Bee Road and follow the signs to Dingmans Falls Visitor Center.

Do not miss this attraction. At the visitor center, pick up a trail brochure and follow the trail a few steps to exquisite Silver Thread Falls as it slides down a narrow rock chute. The trail leads on for ¼ mile further

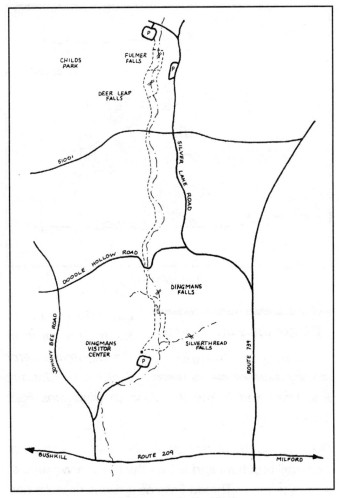

Dingmans Falls Trail

to the powerful Dingmans Falls, with railings leaning right over the brink.

GEORGE W. CHILDS RECREATION SITE TRAIL

½ mile

Location: From the traffic light at Dingmans Ferry, follow Route 739 west for 1.2 miles; turn left on Silver Lake Road. Follow Silver Lake Road for 1.6 miles, and turn left into a large parking lot.

George W. Childs Recreation Site is a fine picnic area along a beautiful stream. The trail is well built, with boardwalks and railings overlooking the falls and crossing the stream. It takes you past magnificent Fulmer Falls, the daring Deer Leap Falls, Factory Falls and smaller cascades.

ADAMS CREEK TRAIL

1½ miles

Location: Follow
Route 209 north 1.2
miles from the light
at Dingmans Ferry.
Park along an old road on the east side of Route 209.

From the parking area, use extreme caution and cross
Route 209, then follow the old road on the south side
of the creek up to the first pool and waterfall. Hiking
beyond this point is *not* recommended.

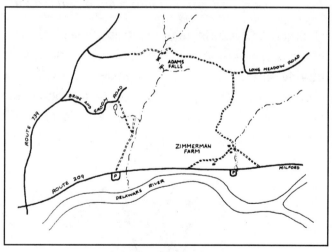

Adams Creek Trail

INDIAN POINT TRAIL
½ mile

Location: *From the Dingmans Ferry light, proceed north on Route 209 for* 4.4 *miles to an exposed shale outcropping. If coming from the north, the outcropping is 0.7 mile south of Raymondskill Road. There is parking in the level area behind the road that slants upwards.*

Follow the road up, past a small slide, to where it makes a right hand turn at the crest of the rim. Blue blazes lead right from this turn along the crest to the highest point, known as Indian Point.

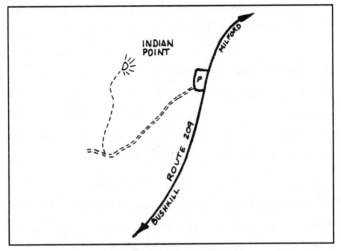

Indian Point Trail

<table>
<tr><td>

RAYMONDSKILL FALLS TRAIL

¼ mile

</td><td>

Location: *From the Dingmans Ferry light, proceed north on Route 209 for 5.1 miles, and turn*

</td></tr>
</table>

west on Raymondskill Road. Follow the road for 0.4 mile to a parking lot on the left.

There are two trails leading to the top and bottom of the falls, with a connecting trail between them. The paths are slightly rough, so use caution here. The falls

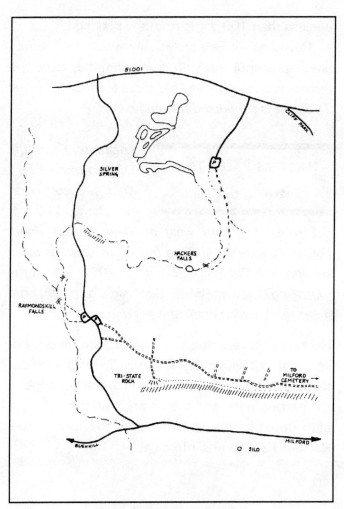

Raymondskill Falls Trail

are less than 100 yards from the parking lot.

Raymondskill Falls are usually awesome. The falls are a powerful straight drop, and they create a throaty roar. Don't stand too close to the edge! ***Note: This area is scheduled for renovation.***

HACKERS FALLS TRAIL
¼ mile to falls

Location: *From the Dingmans Ferry light, proceed north on Route 209 for 5.1 miles, and turn west on Raymondskill Road. Follow Raymondskill Road for 1.7 miles to its intersection with Old Milford Road (SR 2001), and at the "Entering Delaware Water Gap" sign, turn right onto a dirt road, which ends at a parking area.*

Hackers Falls resembles more of a giant faucet, not very high but with gushing power. To reach the falls, follow the old road which begins at the left edge of the parking area, and then branch off right along a path down to the stream below the falls, where Hackers Falls churns into a pool.

The Delaware River

Beginning at Mashipacong Island north of Milford and ending at Arrow Island in the Gap, approximately 38 miles of the Delaware River flows within the boundaries of the Delaware Water Gap National Recreation Area. Maps, information and safety tips about the river are available at Park Headquarters and at the visitor centers.

Under Park Service regulations, canoe camping is permitted when the distance being traveled is too great to be covered in one day. The camping areas are designated by the symbolic sign for canoe camping. The rapids on this stretch of the river are less than Class II ICF/AWA (three-foot waves, clear channels, maneuvering required). High water and cold water will increase the river difficulty one class. Several canoe liveries offer services in the area. They can be located in the yellow pages or from lists available at Park Service offices.

A canoe averages 2 to 3 miles per hour on the river. Popular day trips are from Milford to Dingmans Ferry, 8 miles; Dingmans Ferry to Bushkill, 10 miles; Bushkill to Smithfield, 8.5 miles; and Smithfield to

Kittatinny, 6.5 miles. An early start or an overnight trip could allow coverage of two or three sections.

Fishing is quite popular in the Delaware, either from bank or boat. Trout are found within the tributaries, such as the Flatbrook in New Jersey and Bushkill Creek in Pennsylvania. Look for pickerel, sunfish and rock bass in the adjacent lakes and ponds. The Delaware itself contains carp, catfish, shad, smallmouth bass, muskellunge and walleye. For fishing in Pennsylvania, you need a license if you are 16 or older; in New Jersey, a license is required if you are 14 or older. Pennsylvania licenses may be obtained at most sporting goods stores, from county treasurers, and at Fish Commission regional offices. New Jersey licenses may be obtained from county and municipal clerks and at most sporting goods stores. A reciprocal agreement between the two states allows the holder of a license from either state to fish in the Delaware River or from its banks. This agreement does not apply to tributaries leading to the river.

MILFORD TO DINGMANS FERRY

8 miles

Begin just north of the Milford bridge. The main channel flows on the west side of Minisink Island and Namanock Island. Island camping is available on both. Sandyston Canoe Camp is located on the New Jersey shore south of Namanock Island. The remains of an old eel weir is evidenced by the rock ''dam'' just north of the Dingmans Ferry bridge. Dingmans Access is on the Pennsylvania side below the bridge.

DINGMANS FERRY TO BUSHKILL

10 miles

A long stretch of riffles lies just south of Dingmans Access. It is a popular fishing area of osprey during the spring. Hornbeck Canoe Camp lies on the Pennsylvania shore at the south end of the riffle. The main flow of the river is on the east side of Shapnack Island, where island camping is available. A fairly good set of rapids is found below Shapnack Island, next to the New Jersey shore. Mostly quiet water leads to a limited access at Eshbacks on the

Pennsylvania side. Buck Bar Island provides island camping. Shore camping is available at Toms Creek and Valley View on the Pennsylvania shore. A small area for camping on the New Jersey shore south of Valley View and north of Bushkill Access is a nice mid-point stop.

BUSHKILL TO SMITHFIELD

8½ miles

Peters and Quinn Campsites are located on the New Jersey shore south of Bushkill. The river makes an "S" curve south of Peter's Area. This location is one of the most scenic on the river. Hemlocks on high mountains line the Pennsylvania shore, and a rock formation resembling five loaves of bread might be seen on the Pennsylvania side at water's edge. A few sets of fairly good rapids lead to Sambo Island, where camping is permitted, and to Hamilton Canoe Camp on the New Jersey shore. Depending on the water levels, high-speed power boats may be seen in this area. In the next section of the river, camping is allowed on Depew Island, but not on Poxono Island. Power boats frequent this area, and special channels have been established for canoes and other non-powered boats.

Smithfield Beach Access is on the Pennsylvania shore near the end of the channel.

SMITHFIELD TO KITTATINNY POINT

6½ miles

This portion of the river receives high visitor use by anglers, power boats, tubers, etc. Tocks Island (part of Worthington State Forest) provides island camping. Labar Island (also part of Worthington State Forest) provides the last camping area before the Water Gap area. The large Depue Island is privately owned. Worthington State Forest campground, office and boat ramp are located on the New Jersey shore across from Shawnee Inn. The large Shawnee Island on the Pennsylvania side is also private. The large pilings in the river near the southern end of the island are the remains of a railroad bridge. The I-80 bridge is just north of Kittatinny Point Access and the Water Gap. Due to heavy use by power boats, a channel for canoes and other non-powered boats has been established here.

OTHER ACTIVITIES

There are opportunities for various other recreational activities within the National Recreation Area. Hunting and fishing are allowed within the area in accordance with state regulations. There are several campgrounds within and adjacent to the Recreation Area. Special regulations apply to camping on the Appalachian Trail and Delaware River.

Rock climbing is popular in the Gap area, as is ice climbing in the winter. A snowmobile trail is located nearby at Smithfield Beach. Sightseeing by car or bicycle is always popular along the less-traveled roads through the park. There are several picnic areas and two lifeguarded beaches in the summer. Park rangers lead nature hikes and canoe trips according to posted schedules. Some historic houses in the area have been restored and are open for visitation on a scheduled basis. Millbrook Village Days and Peters Valley Crafts Festival are two special annual events.

THE NEW YORK-NEW JERSEY TRAIL CONFERENCE

The New York-New Jersey Trail Conference is a non-profit federation of 82 hiking and outdoor clubs and more than 9,000 individual members working together to build and maintain trails and promote conservation.

The Conference was formed in 1920, when local hiking clubs gathered to plan a system of marked trails to make Bear Mountain-Harriman State Parks more accessible to the public. In this same area, Trail Conference founders constructed and opened the first section of the Appalachian Trail in 1923. During the 1930's, more trails were built, and a system of  trail maintenance was developed, giving each hiking club a share of the responsibility. Today, this maintenance network covers more than 1,000 miles of marked trails from the Catskills and Taconics south to the Delaware Water Gap.

Activities are carried out almost entirely by volunteers who work together to advance these common goals:

— building and maintaining trails and trail shelters in the metropolitan area of New York and New Jersey.

— promoting public interest in hiking and conservation.

— aiding in the protection of wildlands, wildlife and places of natural beauty.

In addition to trail building and maintenance, volunteers of the Trail Conference have devoted many hours to current projects and issues affecting the trails. Every spring, the Conference sponsors Litter Day, a massive effort to clean the trash out of our woods. Nearly a thousand people participate in this event, carrying out tons of litter from the trails. Recent projects of Trail Conference members include extending the Long Path in New York and local management planning for the Appalachian Trail in New York and New Jersey.

Conference publications include the *New York Walk Book*, the *Appalachian Trail Guide for New*

York-New Jersey, the *Guide to the Long Path*, *Hiking the Catskills*, *Harriman Trails*, and maps for Bear Mountain-Harriman State Parks, North Jersey Trails, East Hudson Trails, West Hudson Trails, Kittatinny Trails, High Mountain, Pyramid Mountain, the Hudson Palisades, the Shawangunks and the Catskills, as well as the *Trail Walker*, a bi-monthly newspaper for members. For further information about the Trail Conference, call or write:

NEW YORK-NEW JERSEY TRAIL CONFERENCE
GPO Box 2250
New York, NY 10116

(212) 685-9699